A Woman's Guide to Training Her ~~Dog~~ Man

By

Stephanie Brigham-Brock

Disclaimer

All the material contained in this book is provided

for educational and informational purposes only.

No responsibility can be taken for any results or

outcomes resulting from the use of this material.

To my son, Paris, who has always been an extraordinary boy. May he grow to become an amazing man for an amazing woman one day.

TABLE OF CONTENTS

SECTION ONE:
CARING FOR YOUR MAN.........27

INTRODUCTION

Hello, Beautiful! Did you do a double take before picking up my book? I'm sure you're a dog-lover if it caught your attention.

I see you thinking…

"Is she calling my man a dog?"

"Is she saying my man should be treated like the dog he is?"

"Is she saying a dog and my man are exactly the same?"

Let me assure you, I'm saying none

of those things exactly but a combination of all of those things partially.

I know your man isn't a dog. And, hopefully, he doesn't behave like a dog.

What I'm saying is, we treat our dogs very well, indeed. We love them with our whole hearts. We pamper them, we easily forgive them, and we respect their needs.

So, stay with me here. Just imagine treating your man like you treat your dog. Yes? Yes!

It's an intriguing concept, is it not?

Take a moment to consider this idea, and then take my book home with you and try my well-thought-out and heavily road-tested ideas. I can promise you this: If you practice the suggestions I present in this book, two things will happen:

• First and foremost, you'll have a happy, appreciative man in your life.

• Second—and most importantly—you (my deserving beauty) will be a happy and satisfied woman.

Men are naturally happy when you treat them well. In his happiness, your man will be inspired to pamper you, which will, in turn, make you happy in your own right.

Forget about the popular argument about men having all sorts of reasons that make their life worthwhile. The sole reason a man lives is to make his woman happy. And almost everything he does points to his determination—and sometimes his desperation—to attract and keep the attention of a female.

We all know—but would rather not admit—that men are simple creatures. We, on the other hand, are the complicated ones. Men are built to be simple and fun-loving.

The trick to managing them is to treat them well. If you learn how to treat your man right, he'll give you whatever you want!

So, how about treating your man like you treat your dog?

You really love your dog, and you never hesitate to show it. That's why your dog is your best friend.

The same can be true of your man. If you treat your man like you treat your dog, he'll become your best friend, too. You know the saying, "A man's best friend is his dog." The reason he chose his dog as a best friend over you is because you're not treating him well, or at least not with the same kind of care with which you treat your loving pooch.

Every dog that's treated well ends up being amazing. Such dogs are loving, kind, devoted, extremely protective, and loyal. This is because we treat them with love, respect and kindness—the same things you should lavish on your man.

You strive to fulfill each and every one of your dog's needs. You speak to him gently and with respect. He has the best food. Your love for him is expressed openly with cuddling and rubbing and scratching his head, back, and tummy.

Notice how you effortlessly maintain that eye contact while speaking to your dog and exclaiming how he's such a 'good boy." These are tested and proven ways in which we, the female folks, have treated our dogs really well over time. However, we'll definitely have it better with the male folks if we treat them the same way we treat our dogs.

And this is what this book will give you. It will tell you how to apply effective tweaks and adjustments so your man will give you the same enthusiastic love you enjoy from your dog. In this book, I provide the "what to do," "how to do it," and "what to expect."

It's a complete package of wisdom, and one you'll be so glad you have!

So, let's begin. This book is divided into three sections, each section representing a core aspect you need to connect with in your man, presented in the most effective order.

Ready? Here we go!

SECTION ONE

CARING FOR YOUR MAN

This first section of this book is dedicated to teaching you how to care for your man.

Basically, it's all about learning his love language—that is, learning what makes your man feel loved. You'll learn how to show him you appreciate and respect him, and you'll discover the power of praise. But first, you'll learn how

to identify and care for his basic needs,
which will inspire your man to bring you
his heart on a platter.

SECTION TWO
TRAINING YOUR MAN

In this section, you'll learn how to make your man do your bidding—and you'll hardly have to lift a finger. By applying the lessons you learned in Section One, you'll win his loyalty simply by taking care of all his basic needs.

So, consider this section as basic training. Yes, you heard right—basic training. I'll ask you to think of five things that you'd love your man to always do for you, anywhere and any time. And then I'll tell you how to train him to do these five things. This is just for starters, of course, but you'll see how easy this training can be.

Whether it's around the house, in the bedroom, or out in public, you have the power to inspire your man to do sweet things for you. The prerequisite is taking care of his basic needs. Once you do that, you'll be surprised at how very trainable and coachable he is. Happiness is yours, and your man is the one who will bring it to you! Give him what he wants, and he'll always give you what you want.

The power is in you, so use it! You're sitting on a goldmine. And your goldmine isn't just your sexy physical self. Your goldmine is also in your head.

So, we're going to learn how to use that big brain of yours to train and coach your man into tip-top shape so he can treat you like you deserve to be treated.

SECTION THREE:

CREATING A FUN-LOVING
RELATIONSHIP WITH YOUR MAN

The previous two sections gave you the keys to unlock the treasures in this section. If properly used, these keys will get you everything you want from your relationship. You've put in the work, and now you have your man eating out of the palm of your hand. He now treats you with the love, respect, and kindness you deserve.

We all know that anything worth having requires a considerable amount of effort. A man who's emotionally and physically healthy can be turned into an extraordinary man with just a little extra work.

Here's the first key: Men are simple. They want and need very little, at least compared to us.

So, come along with me and learn how to create an extraordinary man that you'll be proud to call your own.

SECTION ONE
CARING FOR YOUR MAN

Like your dog, your man will become your best friend if you treat him well. If you treat your man with the care you give your dog, he'll love you, cuddle with you, and protect you. But you have to be patient with him and always show him that you truly respect him.

More importantly, you need to understand that this is a process, and it will take time. As with most transformations that last, there's no quick fix. But this doesn't mean the process is difficult or complicated. You start by taking care of your man's basic needs.

BASIC NEEDS

A man, like a dog, has pretty basic needs—good food, hydration, restful sleep, and daily (fun) exercise. These are the needs you must meet to ensure your man stays healthy and happy.

Making it fun is critical. Men love and need fun, especially after a hard day at work. So, just like taking your dog to the park to play, think of fun activities to share with your man.

A man needs to feel necessary and

loved. If you let your man know he's at the core of your loving family, that sense of importance will make him your loyal friend forever.

Now, let's look at each of these basic needs one at a time.

BASIC NEED I
GOOD NUTRITION

We've all heard the old saying, "The way to a man's heart is through his stomach." This is actually still true. In fact, it's been tested and proved. Men love to be nurtured, and feeding your man good food is the most elemental form of nurturing.

There's always a healthy way to prepare even the most 'not so healthy' foods. We now know that healthy foods don't just build muscle and prevent us from gaining weight. They offer so much more than this to our well-being.

Eating healthy foods can reduce the risk of heart disease, including heart attacks and stroke. Eating healthy foods may also protect the body from certain types of cancers and type-2 diabetes. Good food also keeps your man fit, so he'll look great in and out of his clothes—which, by the way, is good for you.

Find out what your man loves to eat, and then find a healthy way to prepare it.

We love to see our man looking healthy and fit. This keeps us more attracted to him. Such strong attraction ultimately leads to increased intimacy between the two of you, which is greatly beneficial to you both.

Studies have shown that good nutrition will reveal your man's hidden six-pack abs—and his sexy Bedroom Beast at the same time.

The right foods—like tuna, egg yolks, Alaskan king crab, and low-fat milk with vitamin D—can increase testosterone levels, which translates to better erections and healthy sperm. Optimum testosterone levels enhance a man's performance in the bedroom. If he pleases you intimately, it will enhance his self-esteem and ultimately make him happy, which in turn, will make him want to make you happy, too.

Remember, your man wants to please you. And the more he's able to please you sexually, the more he'll want to please you outside the bedroom in other areas of your lives. When a man can make his woman happy, he feels masculine, he feels strong and protective. He feels joy and happiness for having a woman he can satisfy and call his own at the same time. As a result, he takes responsibility for taking good care of you at all times. If you can follow me on this and take action, you'll see that this is some powerful stuff.

Take good care of your man, and he'll take good care of you. By feeding your man well with nutritious food, you'll receive love, respect, and kindness in return.

BASIC NEED II
MAKE FOR HIM A SPECIAL PLACE,
A PLACE OF HIS OWN

To show our love for our dog, we often dedicate a special place for him in our home. In such a space, he can rest, relax, and play. Often, to create this nest of comfort, we put in a considerable amount of effort.

First, we head to an upscale pet store to find our dog a soft, comfortable bed and a snuggly blanket to match. Then we painstakingly pick out several interesting toys for our pet so he has the important experience of CHOICE and can find his favorites among this pool of toys.

Just like your dog, your man would love a comfortable and special place of his own.

Your man would love a place to sit and unwind in maximum comfort. Perhaps this means finding him a special chair that supports his body in just the right position or a side table that holds his favorite after-work drink? How about a special pair of casual slippers to comfort his tired feet in the evenings?

He'll appreciate having a place outside, too, where he can sit and smoke his favorite cigar or drink a glass of wine on weekends. Or maybe your man's idea of relaxation is to sit in front of one of those monstrous television screens watching his favorite sports or news show. Whatever his needs or wants, why not provide them for him as you would for your loving pooch?

Most importantly, let this space be his and his alone. Don't fuss to arrange things or tidy them up in your man's sacred space. Don't interfere with him at all unless he invites you to.

A man deserves a place of his own, just like you do.

We, as women, can be overly sensitive and sometimes feel left out when we don't get constant attention from our men. Believe me, even if your man seems lost in his own thoughts, that doesn't mean he doesn't adore you or love spending time with you. It just means that he, like everyone else—including your dog—needs some time and space alone to unwind, to think, to just be. Having his own special, peaceful space to do this is a loving gift.

And of course, spending time in his special place gives him the opportunity to miss you and recognize how amazing you are. So, you can see why it's so vital to give him some (space) at all cost.

BASIC NEED III
DAILY EXERCISE

To stay healthy and fit, your dog needs exercise on a daily basis, and so does your man. Many men love to go to the gym, play basketball, golf, soccer, or go for a run in the park. Just like your dog enjoys the dog park and hanging out and playing with other dogs, your man loves having that exercise/play time with his buddies.

Don't think your man must or needs to spend most of his time with you.

Being away from you will make him appreciate you more and enjoy the time you two do spend together. After all, absence, they say, does make the heart grow fonder. Additionally, when he goes out with his friends to play "man" sports, it's a good way to increase his testosterone level.

Exercising is good for keeping your man's testosterone levels optimal.

Whether he realizes it or not, your man will feel good about himself the more he exercises. Exercise increases testosterone, and testosterone increases his feelings of manliness and his protective instincts toward you. Also, he'll feel the strong urge to please you more in your relationship.

Studies have shown that regular exercise acts like a natural Viagra.

In a study by the School of Medicine at the University of California, San Diego in La Jolla, sedentary, middle-aged men who were put on an energetic exercise plan for nine months were observed to have improved sexual desire, more active sexual function, and better sexual satisfaction. This study also showed a corresponding improvement in their sex lives as their fitness levels improved.

Exercising also enhances your man's self-image. Actually, it does the same for you. Exercising isn't just heart-healthy stuff, it's libido-healthy for you and him. Think of all those things you could try out together if you were both healthy and fit. Fitness is a great way to achieve a healthy and sexy relationship.

After all, feeling sexy plus looking sexy is just damn sexy!

Many of us want our man to be strong, protective, and always in charge. However, what we're actually doing is trying to turn our men into us—we want them to talk about their feelings and hang with us at the mall, among other things. While sharing feelings isn't entirely a bad thing to do, it's important to know that men express themselves differently than we do. I say, your man isn't your girlfriend, so don't treat him like he is.

Sometimes men express themselves in words, but most times they do it without words. When they choose the latter, you might find it hard to decipher these expressions. But don't fret. Chances are high they may not even know themselves what they're trying to convey, but their feelings are genuine.

You can tell a lot by how your man kisses you, his proximity to you, when he seeks important advice from you, smiles at you with his eyes, brings you into his group of friends, is a good listener, and watches out for your welfare. All these are indicators that your man feels absolutely great about you and around you.

BASIC NEED IV
STANDING BY HIM
(ESPECIALLY IN TIMES
OF ILLNESS)

When our dog isn't eating well or his nose feels a little too warm, we get worried. We can tell immediately when he's not wagging his tail like he usually does or isn't as energetic when jumping around or giving us kisses. These changes in behavior let us know that something is very wrong.

When our adorable pooch isn't feeling well, we get him to the veterinarian as soon as possible.

But what do we do when our man isn't feeling well? Perhaps he has a cold, a headache, or he's just feeling like crap for whatever reason. Maybe he curls up on the couch and goes quiet. Do we go to him and ask him what he needs? Do we ask him if he wants to talk? Do we ask him what we can do to make him feel better? Most times, we don't! Our usual reaction is to roll our eyes and think, "There he goes, getting all quiet again." Other times, we silently call him weak and, often, we don't stop at that. We ring up our girlfriends and tell them how our man is acting like a baby again when all he has is a cold. Then we start making it all about us. We remind ourselves and everybody else that when we get sick, we just keep on going. We go on about how much stronger we are than men when we're sick and how we don't lie around acting like we're dying from a common cold.

Ladies, listen up! We have to be careful with these judgments, especially if we voice them. We can destroy our man's ego with just a few words of criticism.

Everyone handles not feeling well differently.

In general, men handle not feeling well differently than women do, just like they handle criticism from their buddies differently. When we're being criticized by our girlfriends, we take those comments very personally, and their words can hurt our feelings for days or even years. Men, on the other hand, take criticism from their buddies simply as a chance to get better. They usually don't take it too seriously. For one, they don't minimize the problem but rather try to understand the reasons why they're being criticized. Also, they typically don't rationalize, make excuses, or try to justify their actions. They take the blame and put whatever message the advice carries to good use. How many women can easily do this? Let's be honest. Not many!

So, back to our sick man on the couch. What if we treat him like we'd treat our sick pooch when he feels bad? What if we let him lay his head in our lap and rubbed his shoulders or scratched his back until he dozed off? What if we got him some chicken noodle soup instead of rolling our eyes and turning away? What if we didn't talk to our girl-friends about his illness and just kept it to ourselves?

We shouldn't speak negatively about the man we've chosen to spend our limited, precious time with. Just the act of not sharing negatives about your man with others makes your relation-ship that much sweeter and stronger.

Your man doesn't want to be sick, but he is. You can help him feel better.

You can help your man get through the 'bad' times with your gentle care and love. He'll appreciate you more for it. And you'll be teaching him through your actions how to take care of you during times when you're not feeling well—emotionally or physically.

BASIC NEED V
KEEPING HIM SAFE FROM HARM

When we go outside with our dog, we keep him on a leash for a number of reasons. A leash helps keep him safe from harm—like running out into traffic or attacking or getting attacked by another dog or even a wild animal. It also keeps him from impregnating our neighbors' dogs. Ultimately, the leash is for the dog's protection and is borne out of our love for our dog.

It may sound shocking to say so, but I believe we should have a virtual leash on our man as well. Why? For the same reasons we use one on our dog—to protect him because we love him.

The virtual leash isn't a physical restraint, of course. It's invisible. We put it on our man each time he leaves the house. The virtual leash is made of our caring thoughts, kisses, and hugs. It carries the memory of the special place you've made just for him in your home.

It conveys your genuine concern and affection and transmits the memory of how you're his woman—the one that allows him his free time. It reminds him that you regard him as your man, not your girlfriend. This invisible leash constantly reminds him of how he's allowed to go out with friends without you complaining or whining about it. It connects you to him in a way that lets him know you're a partner who wants him to enjoy his sports, his cigar, or even an after-work beer, alone or with his buddies.

In this invisible love-leash lingers your body's scent when you're snuggled up to him in bed.

See the leash as your Lasso of Truth, and see yourself as Wonder Woman.

Wonder Woman has the Lasso of Truth as her primary weapon and tool. This magical, golden lariat allows her to force anyone to do her bidding effortlessly.

Wonder Woman demonstrates a remarkable level of skill with her lasso. She can create air currents just by twirling it or combine it with her speed and strength to go on the offense or defend against any enemy.

Fascinating, isn't it? But what's more interesting is that you can turn this invisible love-leash into your own Lasso of Truth to get your man to do your bidding.

This invisible love-leash represents the love he feels for you. This virtual leash always pulls him away from danger and back home to you. Maybe the reason so many men spend a lot of time away from home is because they're not wearing their love-leash. It could be that men have affairs with other women because we haven't applied the invisible love-leash.

I guarantee that the woman he's

having an affair with has applied her love-leash, since yours is wanting. She's taking good care of your man. His needs are being met and, in return, you better believe he's fulfilling her wants and needs.

But we don't need to go to that unhappy scenario. Once you've put the virtual love-leash on him, he'll keep himself out of harm's way and walk himself home every time.

Just like your dog is so happy to see you every day when you come home because you treat him so well, your man will feel the same. He'll look forward to being with you and treat you like the treasure you are.

Now, with all these tasks you're being assigned, you may be wondering what the heck you're getting out of this deal. Trust me. You'll be receiving all the love and affection you want from your man because you've stepped up your game by giving him everything he needs to feel comfortable and cared for. Now he's well prepared for the next phase, in which you'll train him how to treat you the way

you want to be treated.

SECTION TWO

TRAINING YOUR MAN

Having ensured that your man's basic needs are met, you can now train him on how to treat you. Consider this: Imagine your dog not being fed regularly or receiving regular exercise. Wouldn't this neglect affect his wellbeing?

Of course it would!

Here's another scenario: What if your dog's sleeping area was infected with fleas? If he was scratching and miserable, wouldn't it be hard to train him to sit, stay, roll over, or catch? Absolutely! The poor thing could barely sleep in those conditions. However, by meeting all his basic needs, you've already designed an enabling environment for his training.

One of the main basic needs you've met is that your dog feels safe with you. Your dog knows he can trust you and that you truly care about him; hence, he has no problem doing whatever you ask him to do. The same goes for your man.

Meet his basic needs first, build his trust, and then he becomes trainable, coachable, and open to instructions.

Before embarking on this journey of teaching your partner, it's important that you identify the type of relationship you want with him. You have to figure out what's important to you in that relationship. Fine-tuning these details is the foundation of the learning process. When you're training or teaching your man how you want to be treated, you have to be clear. If you give him mixed messages, he'll get it all wrong. Know what you want from him, and be crystal clear on how you want him to treat you. And, importantly, be sure you stick to these principles and never go back on them unless you discuss this change with him first.

For instance, say you're training your dog to stay off the couch and then one evening you invite him onto the couch to snuggle with you because you desire his company. You come home from work one day and find him on the couch. Furious, you command him to get down. You can see how the poor dog is getting mixed messages on what you want from him, and that's not fair. You need to decide if you want him on the couch or not at all times and stand by your decision.

This is no way to train a dog, and you certainly can't train your man this way, either.

Many of us give our men mixed messages. We can be complicated, especially when our emotions change. There's nothing wrong with this. After all, we are who we are. But we need to take into account that most men get confused by this. Men like simplicity. If they find something that works for them—say a toothpaste, a shaving cream, a specific workout routine, or a suit designer—they stick with it for as long as possible. That's why they have no problem wearing the same pair of blue jeans over and over again for years.

Women, on the other hand, will find a makeup they feel works perfectly for them, and then they'll go out and buy an entirely different makeup for the sake of trying something new. We love to try different workout routines, and we're capable of changing our diets three or four times a year just to see what will happen. We buy new shoes monthly, even though we have 40 pairs in our closet. We patronize different designers even though we have a designer brand that suits our body perfectly. This is just the nature of a woman.

The point is, we women are complex and, because men are simpler, we can't throw all our complexities at them at once. You can't say you want him to treat you a certain way in January and then decide you want him to treat you differently in March. This will confuse and likely aggravate him, and that's the worst approach for training your man properly. You must get clear on what you want and keep it simple.

For most women, there are some things that are 'super-important' to us. For example, I don't like sharing a bathroom with my man. I like having my own bathroom space to do all my weird things in private. My bathroom space is super-important to me. You, on the other hand, may enjoy brushing your teeth side by side with your man in the mornings.

So, now I'm going to ask you to identify five things that are super-important to you—five things that, if your man learned and followed, would make you extremely happy. But first, you must get clear on what you really want from him. You must be clear on what makes you feel happy, respected, and loved. Write down everything that comes to your mind, even if you come up with 50 things. Once you have your list, whittle it down to the five that are most important to you now. We'll start by training your man on just those five important things first, and then, once he has these mastered, we can add more. We want to keep it simple.

Most importantly, be patient and consistent in each of your training points.

All right, honeychild, let's move forward into Basic Training, so we can train this man to treat you like the goddess you are.

BASIC TRAINING POINT I
HOME TRAINING

One of the first things we teach our dogs is home training. "Don't pee and poop in the house," or "pee and poop in the appropriate place(s) (such as wee-wee pads) in the house." Once your dog is trained in such a manner, you immediately have a better relationship.

`You're no longer anxious when he's not within your reach or sight. You no longer have thoughts of him doing his business on your bed or lifting his leg to pee in one of your Gucci pumps. When your dog is finally trained in the art of knowing where and how to do these essential functions, peace reigns between the two of you.

You and your man want to live together in peace and harmony, too. I always think of the home as the woman's domain. Usually, she makes most of the decisions about what, how, and where things go on, in, and around the home. Once a man has managed to get his special chair, TV, closet, and office space, he's usually pretty satisfied. Again... pretty simple stuff.

The woman is left to concern herself with every other thing. So, identify what's important to you. Is a 'no shoes in the house' rule important? Do you want to have dinner in the dining room every night? Do you want to share a bathroom with your man or would you prefer to have a bathroom to yourself? Toilet seat down, or are you flexible? Dirty clothes in the hamper or in the washer? TV in the bedroom or not? Holding hands in public? Kissing only in private? Standing when you leave the table at a restaurant to go to the restroom, or not?

Whatever your preferences, you can tweak the situation to work for your benefit by simply making your wishes clear. You can't have everything your way, but you can certainly choose JUST FIVE, simple rules that are super important to you and that your man won't mind following.

Here are five rules that are important for me:

1. Generosity. I love my man to be generous—especially when it comes to his time with me. I enjoy it when he puts his phone away when we're on our date night. It makes me feel loved when he recognizes those times are just for us to enjoy one another. I appreciate him

being generous with his money, and not just with me. I have a lot of respect for my man when he gives a homeless person a few bucks.

2. Chivalry. I'm a real old-fashioned type of girl. A real lady. I feel cared for when my man opens my car door and stands when I leave the table. I like my chair pulled out and my napkin placed in my lap. I feel loved when we hold hands and exchange sweet kisses, wherever we are.

3. Private time for me. I enjoy hav-

ing my space to read and think. I like it when my man allows me my own personal time when I need or want it.

4. Order. I need order in my living space. I really appreciate it when my man takes his shoes off at the door. I like that he helps keep our living space in the beautiful order I've arranged for our peaceful enjoyment.

5. No radio on in the car. When I'm with my man, I enjoy communicating with him. I don't want to compete with a blasting or chattering radio when

I'm listening to him talk about his day or his dreams or his concerns. What's going on with my man is important to me, so I want to give him 100% of my attention when we're together. And, of course, I expect the same from him.

So, there you have five of my most important rules to live by. Maybe they'll inspire you in coming up with your own.

As long as you've taken care of his basic needs, he'll be happy to do these five crucial but simple things.

Are you getting this yet?

Let me put it simply: You take care of him, and he'll take care of you the way you want him to. Isn't that all we really want from our men? And, just like when you take good care of your pooch, he's happy and behaves himself. He pees and poops in the right place, and he gives you those wet doggy kisses. The same will happen with your man. You take good care of him, and he'll love on you and give you sweet, wet manly kisses.

BASIC TRAINING POINT II
PLAYING NICE FOR TREATS

When our dogs play nice by not barking excessively or biting other dogs or people or not peeing on our Persian carpets, we reward them with a yummy treat for being such a good pooch.

Well, honeychild, just like you reward your dog, you need to reward your man when he follows the five simple rules you've set for him.

Rewards can come in many forms. One is giving him kisses and hugs. Another is preparing and serving his favorite meal. Being appreciative is also a way to reward him for his good behavior.

Show appreciation to your man for remembering to remove his shoes before entering the house. Let him know how much it helps you when he puts his dirty laundry in the appropriate place. Love on him for always being on time for dinner each night. Acknowledge him for caring about you enough to follow your five simple rules. And, give him his most favorite treat (perhaps waking him up for a morning quickie) as an extra reward when he's extra good.

The more you acknowledge and reward him, the more he'll continue to follow your sacred rules.

Stay consistent with the rewards, because men, just like dogs, love getting their treats. You must have noticed how, once your dog realizes he gets a treat when he does a trick like standing on his hind legs or shaking hands with you, he'll start doing the trick without you even asking in the hope of getting that treat.

By now, it shouldn't surprise you when I say your man will do the same thing. He'll love following your rules to receive your loving treats. He'll even do more, to get the treats more often, without you asking him.

How about welcoming him home with his favorite drink served graciously right at the door with a big smile? He'll not only feel pampered, but he'll always look forward to coming home every day for a treat like that. He'll do everything he can not to come home late for fear of missing the treat that's become a part of his life.

On the flip side, in the same way you don't reward your dog when he misbehaves, you need to be sure you don't reward your man when he misbehaves.

After all, these rewards are earned for good behavior. He gets your goodies when he's good to you. This is about having a healthy balance of give and take in your relationship.

You treat him well, and he'll treat you well. You reward him for being a good boy, and he takes good care of you, treating you the way you deserve to be treated.

Wondering what you can offer your man as rewards for treating you right? Consider the following:

•Dress sexy for him. A lace teddy and heels is always a great idea.

•Put on his dress shirt with nothing underneath.

•Take him on a surprise romantic dinner.

•Kiss him goodbye and kiss him when he gets home.

•Tell him when he looks sexy, handsome, or fit.

•Buy him nice gifts (of course, you know what he'll appreciate).

•Give him a surprise lap dance.

•Get him great seats to his favorite

sports event.

•Turn one of your date nights into game night and watch the game with him.

•Give him unexpected hugs—and you can scratch his back and head in the process.

•Give him a neck and back massage.

•Give him spontaneous romantic and flirty compliments.

•Spoil him with delicacies, especially homemade cookies (remember, the way to a man's heart is through his stomach).

•Give him more time and attention than usual.

•Tell him often that you love and appreciate him.

•Of course, the best reward is you, naked, wrapped in his arms.

BASIC TRAINING POINT III
LEARNING FUN TRICKS

Training your dog how to do fun tricks serves as a great bonding experience. In this process, you get to know what your dog can or can't learn and what he's really good at. All dogs can't ride ponies and do backflips, but most dogs can master a few simple tricks like rolling over, shaking hands, or playing games like fetch.

Spending quality and intimate time

with your man is an excellent way of bonding as well. There are several fun tricks you can teach your man that he'll gladly perform for you, over and over again. Apart from bonding, these tricks and the time spent on them will give you both tremendous pleasure and satisfaction.

Sexually, there are things we all enjoy. While we enjoy some of these more than others, the bottom line remains that we do enjoy them.

Having fun with your honey in bed is the perfect time to teach him how to pleasure you properly.

Just as you teach your pooch new tricks using patience, understanding, and love, you must be patient with your man during these important lessons. He's not going to know exactly what your sexual desires are unless you guide him with a gentle hand and plenty of patience.

It's a sad fact, but most men don't have a clue about how to pleasure their woman properly. And it's not their fault. No, that fault lies with us, dearies. We need to start speaking up and letting our men know what really turns us on. We need to let them know what makes us happy sexually. But this takes time and patience, especially if you've been in a situation for many years where you've allowed your man to do whatever he pleases in bed. A man's ego can be bruised easily when it comes to pleasuring his woman sexually. So, guide him gently to your needs, and reward him (and yourself) with orgasms.

This change may be hard for both of you at first. There may be some hurt feelings and misunderstandings. But, once you get past this initial stage, you both will be much happier. Besides, he really does want to please you sexually. A man gets major pleasure when he pleases his woman in bed. It makes him feel powerful and masculine when he hears those moans and soft screams from his woman as a result of what he's doing to her body.

And what more wonderful way to get to know each other and become even closer than discovering each other's bodies intimately?

We'll go into training your man in the bedroom in the next part of this book. With what you know so far, you should have yourself a happy and agreeable partner. We might even say that you've made your man feel special in his own home by training him to follow the five simple rules you've given him that make your life more enjoyable. All that's left is for you is to learn a few more ways to enjoy the relationship that you've successfully built. This awaits you in the next section.

Roll over to the next page!

SECTION THREE
CREATING A FUN-LOVING
RELATIONSHIP

Now that your man's basic needs are met and you've outlined a set of fair, uncomplicated, and clear rules that make you happy—and for which he gets rewarded for following—the next thing is to enjoy a long-lasting, fun-loving relationship.

What makes a fun-loving relationship depends on the personalities of the couple and the background they share. However, there are guidelines that are generally applicable to the establishment and maintenance of romantic relationships between two partners, and these are what we'll be discussing in this section of the book. So, let's get to it!

GUIDELINE I

KINDNESS IS GOLDEN

You know you need to be kind to your dog. If you're mean to him, he'll be afraid of you and try to avoid you. There's no fun or love in being afraid. You speak to your pooch in a pleasant voice and spend time sitting with and petting him. Most dogs enjoy petting over all other rewards. Your dog looks to you as his most important person, and you know that if you treat your dog lovingly, he'll reward you with lots of kisses and cuddles.

Your man should be treated like your most important person, too. After all, he's the one you share your life, hopes, and dreams with, so you should feel free to share your fears and disappointments with him as well.

And, this is the person you share your body with. You literally allow his body inside your own, so shouldn't he be the one you trust with your secrets, dreams, and fears? And he'll trust you with the same. Build the highest level of trust with him by trusting him and allowing him to trust you.

You have no reason not to treat your man with as much love and kindness as you treat your dog.

Always speak to your man in a pleasant, respectful voice/tone. Screaming at your man only makes him angry or causes him to raise his voice right back at you. In the worst case, he might go to the extent of shutting you out completely.

Embrace mutuality and equality. Talk to him the way you'd like to be spoken to. If you want to be respected, respect him. If you want to be loved and desired, love and show that you desire him. If you want to be rewarded with nice gifts and affection, give him presents and affection, too. If you wish to be acknowledged and praised for your good deeds, acknowledge and praise him for every good thing he does for you.

The golden rule certainly does apply in a fun-loving relationship with your man. Do unto him as you'd like him to do unto you.

GUIDELINE II

AVOID PHYSICAL OR

EMOTIONAL PUNISHMENT

We never want to hit or scream at our dog. Yelling and hitting him will scare and scar him. It's cruel to ever hit your dog, and doing so could confuse him and make him act out by barking, biting, destroying furniture, urinating in the house, etc. We know it's always best to use positive reinforcement to get our loving pooch to behave in the way we like. We know that instead of punishing him for doing the wrong thing, we should reward him for doing the right thing. Rewarding him eventually gets him to behave well most of the time. Most important, if we continue to reward our dog for doing the right things, we build trust between the two of us.

Just like your dog misbehaves once in a while, your man will misbehave at one time or another, also, as will you. He'll break some of the house rules from time to time, or he'll stay out later than he said he would. He'll drink too much with the boys and may flirt with some woman while in his tipsy state. He may miss the toilet more than a few times and pee on the floor. In short, he's going to screw up once in a while.

But, just like with your pooch, don't start screaming at him. Don't throw your shoes at him. Don't start breaking your dinnerware. Don't belittle him or call him stupid. This type of behavior will only push him away from you. Always speak to him respectfully. Let him know that his behavior makes you feel lonely, disrespected, disappointed, or sad.

Communicate instead of showing anger.

Don't punish him by depriving him of attention, food, kisses, conversation, or sex. Let me reiterate—punishment doesn't build a trusting relationship, and it can tear a strong one apart. Your decision to punish will only build a wall between the two of you.

Instead of going into silent mode or worse, allow your man some time and space to think about what you expressed to him about how his misconduct makes you feel. Then wait for him to voluntarily retrace his steps and try to make amends. When he does, allow him in and let him right his wrongs. Listen to his side of the story patiently, accept his apology, and forgive him. Reward him for doing the right thing by admitting he was wrong and coming to ask for forgiveness. Then give him a little sugar.

This is what keeps you and your man close, connected, and in love. Forgiveness and treating each other with respect is some seriously sexy stuff!

GUIDELINE III

RELAX AND ENJOY

This is the main deal, after all. Enjoyment is sweet after worthy labor. Now's the time to finally enjoy the benefits of the serious work you've put into the relationship with your man.

Don't you just love it when you can go to the park or to the beach and your dog behaves well? He sits when you say "sit" and stays when you say "stay." He's learned how to catch the ball when you throw it, and he brings it back to you on your command. You feel safe letting him meet other dogs and people. You take him for a walk and there's no pulling and tugging on the leash. He's just so well-behaved that the two of you find your time together extremely enjoyable.

The reason he's so well-behaved is

because you've put the work in. His basic needs have been met. His training is complete. He knows he's loved. You—yes, you—have done an excellent job!

I've always thought of women as the goddesses of the earth. We're the bringers of life. We're the ones who give birth and populate the earth. We're sacred, abundant, necessary, beautiful creatures. We're nurturing, caring, creative beings. We're divine and sexy. So many things in life—especially between a man and a woman—are totally in our control. We can choose to bring beauty, peace, and love into our relationships, or we can choose to bring in ugliness, disharmony, and distress. I'm not saying we're in complete control of how our relationships fare, but we have a lot of power to move our relationships in a good direction.

Women too often think that men have the power in relationships. The truth is, we women hold the power. We have the power to invigorate a man, and we have the power to crush him. Like the saying goes, "If the woman is happy, the whole house is happy." And that's the truth!

Men, in their simplicity, need about three things to feel good and complete: Respect, freedom, and intimacy. We women, on the other hand, need about 3,000 things to feel satisfied. Perhaps I'm exaggerating a bit, but you know what I mean. Most of these 3,000 things we need come in the form of shopping, and shopping, and a little more shopping. We also need a number of girlfriends to discuss our ever-changing emotional states with. We enjoy food—and in many varieties. We also crave trying different types of wines to experience their diverse tastes. And how about life's luxuries like kitchen gadgets, cars, and other cool stuff?

We feel entitled to spontaneous romantic dinners and dates. Who says we don't deserve compliments from men we don't know? We're easily carried away by attractive men, and maybe that's why we're so conscious of our own attractiveness. We can be swept off our feet by a natural sense of humor or an orator with strong, word-weaving powers. Apparently, the list of what women really want is inexhaustible.

While I'm not saying we're wrong or bad for being who we are, we're complex beings who are able to decide what type of relationship we want. And this means keeping it simple with our man. Let's keep the complexities for someone that can actually understand them—our girlfriends!

RESPECT, FREEDOM, AND INTIMACY

I've identified **respect, freedom, and intimacy** as the three things a man needs to feel satisfied and complete in his life. I'd be remiss if I didn't include in this book insight into how these three things work to bring satisfaction to our men—and, of equal importance—satisfaction and happiness for ourselves.

RESPECT

There's no doubt that men want to feel respected—most of all by the woman who claims to love him. After all, you do truly respect and adore him or you wouldn't be with him.

One indicator of respect is the way you talk to your man. Always talk to him in a respectful tone of voice. Never yell or talk down to him. Never roll your eyes when he's talking to you or trying to apologize or make a point.

Nothing good can come from the two of you not being able to converse respectfully with one another. So, lower your voice when speaking to your man. It seems counter-intuitive, but by speaking in a calm, soft voice, your man will listen to you. When making your point, endeav-

or to be clear and truthful. Men like little or no drama. You don't have to beat around the bush before making your point. While a little bit of diplomacy is appreciated, overblowing it won't help matters. Basically, keep it short and precise, and he'll definitely get the message.

Another way of showing respect is by giving your man time to himself or to do his own thing. Obviously, no guy wants to spend every waking moment with you. In fact, most men don't like a needy woman. Men respect a woman who has a life of her own outside their relationship. Make sure you always have a fabulous life of your own and aren't stalking your partner. Go out with your friends and enjoy some time after work with your colleagues just like he does. Go on girlfriends' getaways for a few weekends each year. Apart from the fact that this gives your man space, he'll have the opportunity to value your absence and miss you. Give him time and space to miss you and think about how amazing you've been to him and how lucky he is to have you in his life. None of these are possible if you're always around him.

Good public conduct is also important in your relationship. Don't talk down to your man in the presence of family or friends. Never embarrass him in public. This is the last thing you should ever do. You shouldn't criticize, judge, or undermine his authority in public. Respect his communication and assumptions. Avoid interrupting him while he's making a point. And, when he's absent, ensure that you're always respectful when talking about him.

While it's not entirely out of line to tease him while in public, only do so in a good-natured way. Lastly, whatever happens, don't betray your man. Most men find it impossible to forgive betrayals, especially when they're public knowledge.

FREEDOM

Freedom here means the time your

man spends away from you playing with

others or by himself, watching sports or

being outdoors doing sports or out on his boat with the boys drinking beer all day.

Respect the time your man wants to spend away from you. Don't be whiny when he wants to go out with the boys to a sports event on a Friday night. Don't complain if he wants to have friends over every once in a while to watch a major sports event. As long as his need for freedom isn't happening every Friday night, allow him to enjoy a little time away from you.

Besides, you always have that invisible love-leash on him. You can make things happen anytime from the comfort of your home. The love-leash always works, because you take good care of your man. You've ensured that all his basic needs are met. He, in turn, knows how you want to be treated. After all, he's well trained!

Finally, he loves the home you've created for him. He's aware that his home holds all the fun and loving he'll every need, so, no matter where he is or

who he's with, the invisible love-leash
will always pull him home. Because,
YOU ARE HIS HOME.

INTIMACY (SEX)

The most elemental form of intimacy is, undoubtedly, sex. Let's be honest here. Men love sex a great deal more than most women do. Sex has several different purposes for a man. For them, it's not just a means of expressing love and affection to his woman. It's also a release. Sometimes, a man needs sex to relieve stress and tension so he can fall asleep. I'm sure you've noticed that sometimes after your man has an orgasm, he's snoring in under a minute. When a man has an orgasm, his body immediately relaxes and he becomes mellow. At this moment, the only thing he wants is to lie next to you like a big bag of potatoes.

These and many other reasons are why you mustn't deprive your man of good sex. It's one of the potent ways to keep him closer and make him play by your rules.

Even more powerful than the relaxation effect of orgasm for your man is the sight of his woman enjoying herself. Pleasuring her makes him feel more masculine, more powerful, and more confident.

As I've said before, your man really wants to make you happy, especially in the bedroom. We just have to teach him how. We have to teach him how to make love to our bodies and our hearts without making him feel like he's an inadequate lover. Here are some tips on how you can do this:

1. First, you need to let your man know what your body needs to feel satisfied before you can guide him successfully, so spend some time exploring your body on your own so you can teach your man how to pleasure you. Become aware of the parts of your body that make you excited when they're touched. Pick up a few books about sex, experiment, and notice what gets your juices flowing. Take mental notes on what you don't like so you're better able to steer your man in a different direction. Learn at what times

you like your breasts caressed and when you don't. It's perfectly natural to be too sensitive at certain times of the month for your breasts to be touched, but you must know this about yourself so you can explain it to your man. Know thine self first before teaching thine lover.

As a sort of foreplay, always give your man positive feedback on everything he does well. If he's a good kisser, tell him how much you love the way he kisses you. When he brings home your favorite soup from Whole Foods without you asking, praise him for it. Men are always thinking in terms of sex when you say something positive to them. The more positive feedback your man gets from you, the more he feels he makes you happy. A man believes that if he's making you happy in life, he's also making you happy in bed. When you let him know you're happy with him, it's like an affirmation that he pleases you sexually. And, if your man feels confident in his ability to please you, that makes it easier to teach him how you'd like him to better make love to you.

2. Make the teaching about you, not about him learning how to make love to you. Explain to him that you'd like to explore different things with him in bed. Let him know that it's because the two of you have such a healthy sex life that you're ready to explore and experience even more fun with him. Ask him to share some of his fantasies, and then share some of your own. This will gently guide him to want to explore these new sexy positions and experiences with

you without him feeling as though he's been somehow lacking.

3. Remember, good sex takes time and practice. So, when he tries some of these sexy tricks and doesn't get it right the first time, don't point out what he did wrong. Instead, emphasize what he did right. During your lovemaking, guide him gentle by murmuring things like "Yes, that's it," or "a little slower...harder, softer." Or, better yet, let him know how well he's pleasuring you through sounds of pleasure and calling

him "baby." Remember, he wants to please you in bed more than anything else.

4. Continue to reinforce your happiness with his recently acquired skills. This will make him eager to listen to your guidance. When you're out to dinner, whisper to him how your body is still tingling from last night's lovemaking. Text him from work to let him know you can barely wait to see him later. This will make him smile and guarantee that he'll continue to follow your

guidance whenever you're ready to teach him something new. Before you know it, he'll understand what you enjoy in bed, and he'll be delighted to please you every single time.

Another way to keep your man close is to always be well groomed. Even if you're home just lounging around the house, choose silky pajamas instead of a beat-up old tee-shirt and sweat pants. Keep your hair clean and styled. Keep your body clean and creamed. Men love touching soft, smooth skin. If you aren't wearing makeup, at least keep your lips a little glossy. Men love kissing soft, shiny lips. Be confident in your body. Strut your stuff no matter what size you are. Men find confidence sexy. Never say you look or feel fat in front of your man. Leave that conversation for your girlfriends. When you go out to lunch with him, wear those heels with your blue jeans instead of flats or flip-flops. Heels are a huge turn-on to men. Always accentuate your assets. If you have sexy legs, show them. If you have beautiful breasts, present them on a freakin' platter. If you have lovely lips or eyes, accentuate them. Be proud of your beautiful assets. Trust me—every woman has something that's super attractive about her.

BE ATTRACTIVE! BE SEXY!

Being attractive doesn't mean you have the best body or the prettiest face. An attractive woman is a confident woman with an easy smile. She has a curious mind, and she doesn't hesitate to ask questions. She stands tall with her shoulders back and her head held high, because she knows who she is, what she wants, and where she's going. She's comfortable in the company of other women when she's with her man, because he's wearing his love-leash. No Jealously Needed.

She exercises regularly to stay fit. It makes her feel confident and sexy in and out of her clothes. Exercising also makes her feel happy, because it releases endorphin—the 'feel-good' hormone. And believe me, there's nothing sexier than a happy woman.

So, exercise regularly and eat healthy foods that make you feel good in your clothes and in your body. Stay sexy in and out of the bedroom. Stay attractive when you're with your man in the privacy of your home or out with him in public.

Lastly, stay adventurous in the bedroom. Nothing kills romantic like 'boring.'

In short, stay irresistible and put some good loving on your man.

Besides, by continually treating your man with the love and care you give your dog, you can rest assured you've captured his heart and he's not going anywhere!

you do your dog. In the second section, we discussed the best ways to train your man to do your bidding. The third part discussed how you can enjoy the man you've created based on what you learned in the first and second sections of the book.

I'm quite sure that with the knowledge you've gained from this book, you'll be unstoppable in your quest to make your man into what you know he can be. You now know better the best ways to understand him. With this foundation of understanding, you now know how to take care of him. After showering him with love and care, he now trusts and adores you. He's eager and happy to treat you exactly the way you want to be treated. You've learned how to have the relationship of your dreams with your loving man. And don't be surprised if your man is one of those dogs who can always learn new tricks!

EPILOGUE

I intended this book to be a fun and interesting journey. I hope going through this book has been as beneficial for you as I hoped it would be. In the first section, we talked about giving the same love and care to your man that

A note from the author:

You are an Amazing woman. Always know and believe this. Never accept less than what you deserve in life and love. Please be patient enough to wait for what you truly deserve, and be strong enough to let go of old comforts that no longer serve you. You are worthy of a great life and great love.

With Love,

        Steff